CorelDraw Training For
Laser Cutting Machines
With Many Examples

Written By
Abdulkadir Kaşoğlu

CorelDRAW
GRAPHICS SUITE **X6**

Who am I?

Hello everyone, my name is Abdulkadir Kaşoğlu. I was born in 1989 in Malatya. My entire education life has passed in the city I am in. I graduated from The Anatolian vocational high school electronics department. I spent the last 10 years of my life on graphic design. I first met the Coreldraw program to use it with a laser cutting machine in a small business. After that, I founded my own company and worked with laser cutting machines for about 6 years. After that, I started to give training on various platforms and still continue to provide training. I have more than 5,000 students from many countries around the world. I am writing this book with the aim of reaching more people and contributing to more people's business life. I hope that will be useful.

Contents

Why is this book?

I can summarize my purpose in writing this book as follows. Coreldraw is a program generally used in print shops, but this program has many uses and locations. One of them is laser cutting applications. When you want to learn about the program and do research about it, you generally find articles and videos about the features of the program and the printing applications you can do in the program. However, you come across very few materials and educational content about laser cutting.

Here is to show everyone exactly how I want to do this by writing this book, to show how you can use the CorelDraw program for laser cutting and to be more professional with various sample applications.

The content of the book will proceed as follows. By introducing the Coreldraw program, I will not waste your time, because you can learn this from many sources and videos. So I will only work on examples, assuming you know at least a basic level of the program. You will learn how to use the tools by making many examples. Each sample will both speed up your work and provide you with the opportunity to create a new product. While drawing the products, you can change them according to your imagination and create new products. We will improve our product range by making many product examples. I plan to make several samples from each product. I hope it will be a useful book. I wish you good work from now.

About Laser Cutting

Laser cutting machines are machines that can work with many materials. In general, its logic can be considered the same as CNC machines. While CNC machines work with knives, laser cutting machines make their cutting and engraving with laser light. Although there are obvious differences between the two, there are points where laser cutting machines are more advantageous and therefore they are more preferred.

For example, laser cutting machines do not have a cut share in CNC machines. Since it is cut with light, it is not necessary to leave a cut share. Another advantage is that laser cutting machines can cut much more precisely and are much more skilled at engraving. Laser cutting machines can work with many materials such as wood, plexiglass, paper, fabric, and leather. Perhaps this is its biggest advantage. The more material you can use, the more products you can make.

Laser cutting machines are used in a very wide range from shoemakers to metal processing companies. Therefore, the information given in this book will make a great contribution to you in your business life. Each laser cutting machine has its own working order, and the program of each can be different but basically the same. Only their interfaces are different. However, drawings made with CorelDraw are valid for almost all laser machines.

A few important points...

- All features of the CorelDraw program will not be explained in the book. There are only examples of laser cutting machines. The tools to be used for these applications will be explained during the construction of the samples.
- Simultaneous application of the examples shown in the book is necessary for learning projects and tools and will speed up the learning process.
- Applications are mainly used to teach principles. It is possible to produce many products using these principles and techniques.
- Do not hesitate to contact me if you cannot solve or get out of it. My e-mail address: mrgraphizm@gmail.com
- Coreldraw x6 version will be used in the book. However, you can easily draw the same drawings in other versions.

Part 1: Sample Product Studies

Lesson 1: Keychain Base Design

Open a blank worksheet like every CorelDraw study. This page should look like the following.

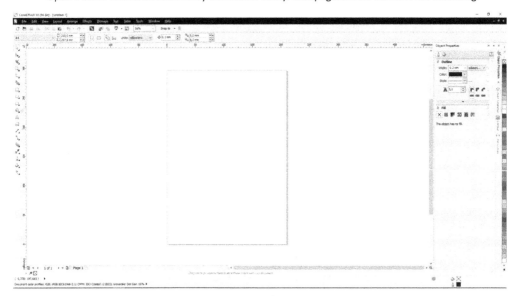

While on this screen, select the ellipse tool (⬭) from the tools on the left side of the program. Then start drawing with left click and hold (CTRL) key to draw a full circle. If you do not hold down (CTRL), you will draw a different ellipse in length and width. The (CTRL) key allows you to draw a circle with an equal length and width. Even if you do not draw with this key, you can make measurements from the adjustment box in the upper left corner. The dimension adjustment part is as shown below.

Since no objects are selected in the image above, the spelling areas are passive. When you select any object, it will show the values in length and width in millimeters.

When you draw the aforementioned circle, the screenshot should be similar to the following.

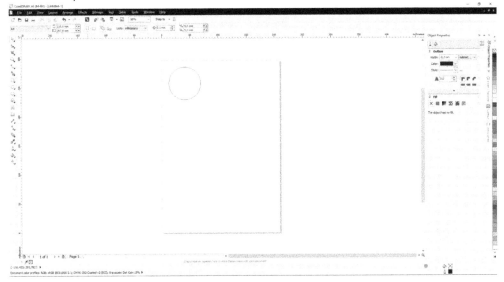

After drawing the circle, pick the selection tool (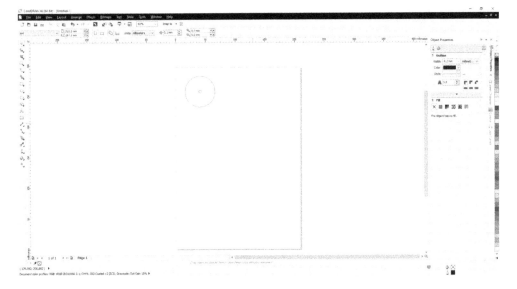) and select the circle and enter the dimensions of 50 millimeters into the dimension box and press enter. Then take the ellipse drawing tool again and hold down the (CTRL) key to draw another circle and adjust its dimensions to 4 millimeters to 4 millimeters. Then take the selection tool and select both objects by clicking and holding from an empty area and center them by pressing the C and E keys respectively. These keys allow both objects to be centered horizontally and vertically. When you do this, your screenshot should be similar to the following. When you draw the aforementioned circle, the screenshot should be similar to the following.

After completing this process, select the small circle you have drawn using the selection tool. After holding the circle with the mouse, hold it with the SHIFT key and move it upwards. Leave it in a place that is not too close to the limit so your key chain base is ready. When you complete the process, the base image will be as follows.

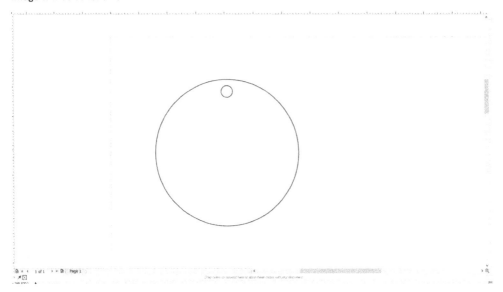

To consolidate and work with different tools and shapes, let's try this on a square.

This time, select the draw rectangle tool ( ) from the toolbar on the left and draw a full square by holding down the (CTRL) key as in the ellipse tool. Your square should look like the following..

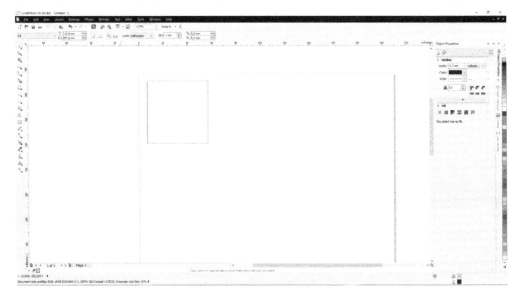

Using the mouse wheel, you can zoom in and out of the area where the pointer is located. Thus, you can control and view the objects you draw more easily. If you want to round the corners after drawing the square, you can do this from the corner edit box at the top. The box is as seen below.

Here, the first option on the left allows you to round the corners. The other provides rounding in from the corner. The last option allows straightening the corners. When you open the lock sign in the middle of the measurements, you can round each corner with different values. When the lock mark is closed, all corners will be rounded with a single value you enter. Let's enter a value here and see the shape the square takes.

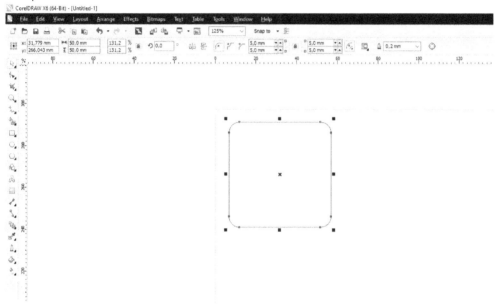

After rounding the corners of the square, you can do the same thing you did for the plate hole in the round object. You can also place it in any of the corners if you wish. For example:

Lesson 2: Carved Keychain Design

Following the keychain base design, you will learn carved keychain design in this lesson. First, draw a circle measuring 50 millimeters by 50 millimeters. Then make the circle smaller by holding it with the mouse from the corner of the circle and holding down the (SHIFT) key, and then copy it by clicking the right mouse button without releasing any keys. When you complete the process, your screenshot should be as follows.

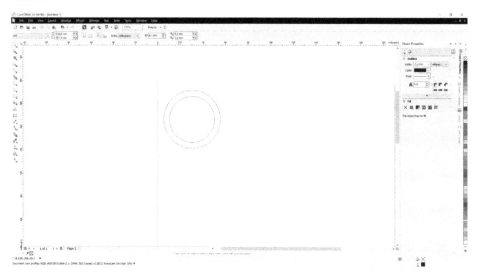

After completing the process, select the two circles that appear on the screen and select the combine tool ( ) from the toolbar at the top so that both circles will merge to form a single object. You can then write a text of your choice by selecting the writing tool. For example, it can be a name or a text. However, make sure that the text or name is short. Because long names or writings will not look smooth and a weak cut will be obtained during the laser cutting stage. After writing the text, you can choose the font you want, and then your screenshot will be as follows.

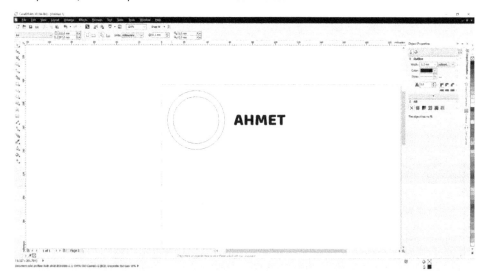

For example, I wrote a name and we need to make some changes to that name. We need to close the space between each letter and combine them into a single object so that the hole in the middle of the letter A does not fall. So we will do the following operations in order. First of all, after selecting the text of Ahmet, we select (convert to curves) option from the Arrange menu or press (CTRL + Q) keys. Thus, we transform the font into a shape. After this process, you may not see any changes in the article, but when you double-click on the article, you will see that it is a shape, not a text anymore. After this process, while

the text is selected, we use the (Break Apart) tool from the toolbar at the top. Thus, we separate each letter of the article and turn it into separate objects. After doing this operation, your screenshot should be as follows.

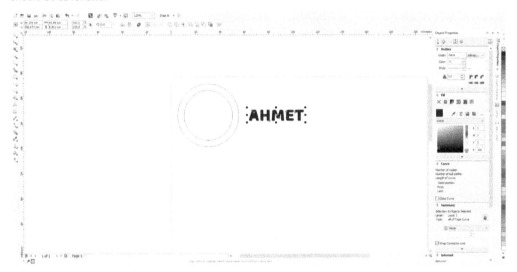

In order to control the article more easily, we select the Outline section as a hairline from the drop-down menu on the right and set the fill section just below it as no fill. If the screen on the right is not open, simply right-click on the selected object and click on properties.

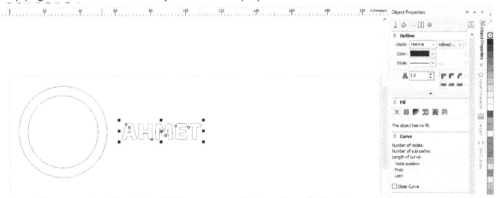

After separating the text and letters, we need to turn these letters into a single object. To do this,

we first select the letter A and select the combine ( ) tool from the toolbar at the top. Immediately afterward, we hold the letter H with the mouse and hold down the (SHIFT) key to the left side, that is, slightly over the letter A, and we shift the other letters to the top of the previous letter. After doing this operation, your screenshot will be as follows.

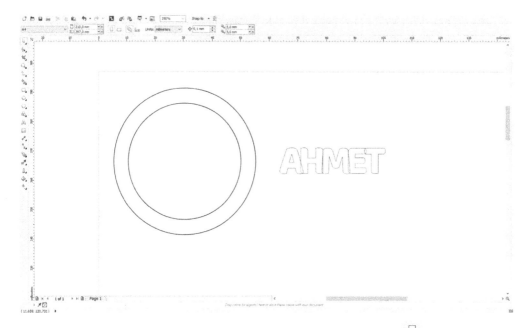

After this point, all you have to do is select all the letters, click on the Weld () tool, and then your text will appear as below.

 Thus, we made the article into a single object. I am adding 1 more name for you and we will have made a keychain named 2. After completing the operation of these two names, place each name in the circles you have previously drawn and adjusted its dimensions to fill the circle. The picture is given below.

After placing the texts as shown in the picture, all you have to do is select all the items and add a few hearts

to use the weld ( ) tool, but to make it a little more animated. Some of the ready-made shapes in the Coreldraw program are one of them in the heart. You can select the heart shape from the shapes menu at the top immediately after selecting the basic shapes winter in the toolbar on the left. The images of both vehicles are shown below.

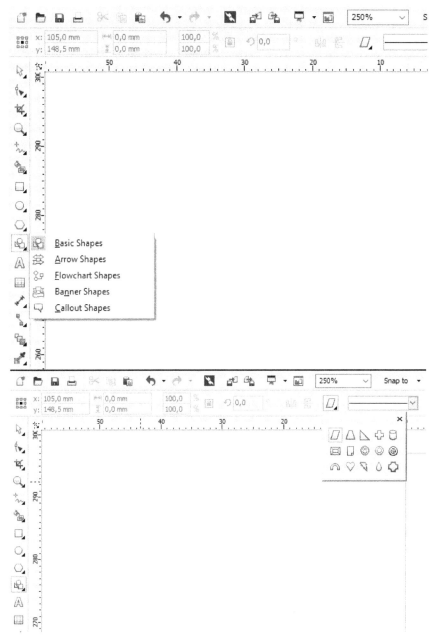

After choosing the heart shape here, you can place the bottom and top of the article by drawing as many hearts as you want according to the size of the space. Just like in the ellipse and rectangle tool, you will get a smoother-looking heart if you draw while holding the (CTRL) key while drawing the heart shape. I share a screenshot by adding a few hearts to the keyring that I just drew.

After doing all these operations, the general drawing of our keychain is ready, only all the objects are combined and creating the necessary hole for the key ring. First of all,

select all items and click on the weld ( ) tool in the top toolbar to make all objects into a single object. After completing the process, take the ellipse tool and hold down the (SHIFT) key and draw a small circle. Select the small circle you have drawn and the key ring and press the C key. The C key here will center your objects vertically. Hold the small circle you draw with the mouse and hold down the (SHIFT) key while aligning it to the top of the key ring. Your drawing should look like the following.

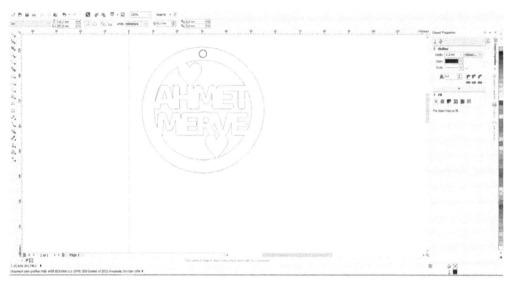

With this last step, your engraved keyring design is ready for the laser cutting machine. You can make the keyring with any material you want. It is completely drawn for cutting.

Lesson 3: Combining Writing and Turning it into a Keychain

In this section, you will only learn how to combine the text and turn it into a keyring. First of all, you need to select a bold font and write a text of your choice. The shape that occurs when you do this is as you see below.

Immediately after writing the article, as in our previous lesson, we repeat the processes that we combined the article into one object. You can adjust the dimensions of your keyring from the size adjustment section on the left side of the toolbar at the top. To repeat; First of all, you should convert the text to shape by selecting convert to curves option from the arrange menu or pressing CTRL + Q. After doing this, you should select the outline, that is, the edge lines as a hairline, and the fill option just below it as no fill from the toolbar on the right. The next step is to select the text and choose the Break Apart tool in the top toolbar to distinguish the letters. After separating the letters, you have to move each letter with the help of the mouse by holding the shift key slightly over the previous letter. After doing all these operations, you should select all the letters and use the weld tool in the upper toolbar to translate the text into a single object. After all these operations, your screenshot will be as follows.

After this process, all you need to do is a very small and easy process. Get the draw rectangle tool from the toolbar on the left. Draw a small square by holding down the CTRL-key. Then draw another square inside this square and select both frames and click on the combine tool in the top toolbar. At the moment, your screenshot should look similar to the one below.

Shrink the squares you draw based on the size of the keyring. Move these two squares just over the top of the text you write. After selecting the squares and the text you wrote, you will be finished by clicking the weld tool on the top toolbar again. The screenshot of the keyring will be as below.

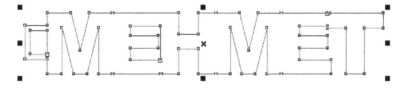

Lesson 4: Making a Keychain by Dressing the Text on the Figure

In this lesson, you will learn how to make key rings by dressing the text on or in the shape. I will do this with a heart shape so that it can be better understood. You can use this technique for any shape you want. I am starting to explain without losing time.

First, select the basic shapes ( ) tool on the left side of the program. After selecting this tool, select the heart shape from the ready drawings box that comes to the top toolbar. The window looks as follows.

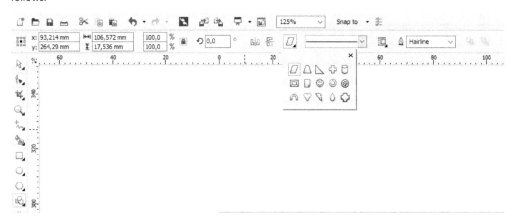

After selecting the heart shape, hold down CTRL and draw a heart with the same aspect and aspect ratio. Draw another small heart inside this heart. Then select these two hearts and click the combine

( ) tool in the top toolbar. This process will combine 2 hearts to make a single, empty object. After the process, your screenshot will be as follows.

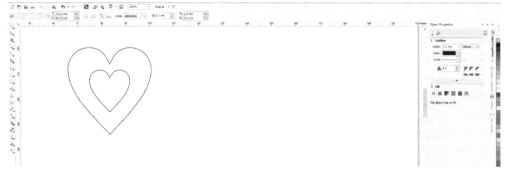

After drawing, write the text you want to put in the heart. After selecting the text, choose Fit Text To Path from the Text menu. Then drag the mouse pointer over the heart. When your pointer lands on the heart, you will see the text sitting according to the shape of the heart. As you move the pointer over the heart, you can make the text come to the desired location. Click on a desired line of the heart. Thus, the text will be placed according to the shape of the heart. After the operation, your screenshot should be as follows.

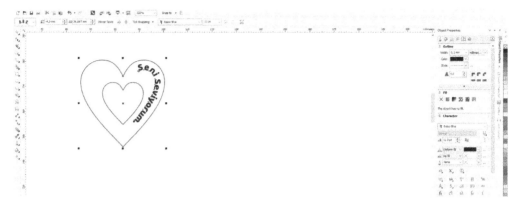

You will see that the toolbar at the top has changed. This toolbar was created to edit the post. The selection box with the ABC text you see at the beginning is the area where you can choose how to dress the text in the shape. You can see how the post has changed by trying different choices. The measure boxes next to it are the part where you can adjust the distance between the text and the shape and the distance from the starting point of the text. The mirror text field is the part where you can reverse the text vertically or horizontally. The next setting is where you can choose the font and size of the post. You can adjust all these settings to your own will. Just like in the article, you can take the shape tool and adjust the letter spacing of the article. In the properties window on the right, you can change the edge thickness and fill the options of the post.

After making these choices, let's draw the hole through which the key chain ring will pass. To do this, take the ellipse tool on the left and draw 2 nested circles and combine these two circles using the combine tool. After finishing the process, place the circles you have drawn so that some amount will come over the junction part of the heart. The screenshot should be as follows.

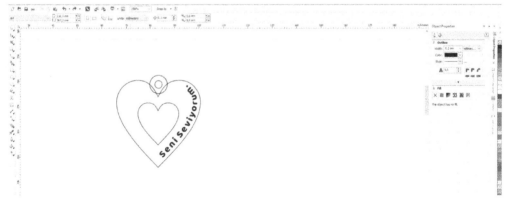

After this step, click on the text you wrote once and turn it into shape by pressing CTRL + Q. Select the circles you have drawn and hold the SHIFT key and click once on the heart shape. Thus, you will have chosen only the circles and the heart. Combine these two shapes using the weld tool. Your heart keychain will be ready. The screenshot will be as follows.

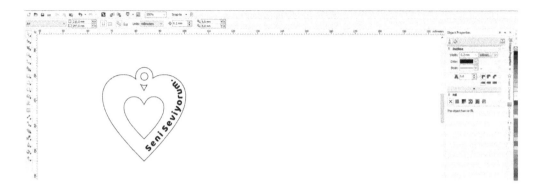

Lesson 5: Making Simple Keychain with Letter Cutting Method.

I made this keyring design for you to learn how to prepare the text for laser cutting. In this lesson, we will first draw the keyring base. To do this, take the rectangle tool on the left and draw a long rectangle. Round the corners of the rectangle by entering the desired dimension in the corner rounding section that I mentioned earlier. When you complete the process, the screenshot will be as follows.

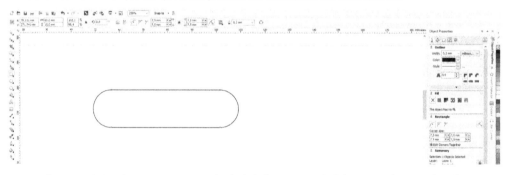

After completing the process, insert a keyhole hole at any end of the rectangle using the ellipse tool. Type a text you want or choose a bold font. After selecting the text, convert it to shape by pressing CTRL + Q letters. At this stage, your screenshot will be as follows.

After this step, there is an operation you need to do for letters with a space in the middle, such as the letter R. Draw a thin and long rectangle for this process. Place it in the middle of the space of the letter R. It should be like the picture below.

Make sure that the rectangle you draw does not overlap with other letters and is placed in the middle of the space. Then select the text and the small rectangle and click the Back Minus Front tool ( ) at the top. Thus, you will cut the letter with a space in the middle. In this way, you can easily use the letters with a space in the laser cutting machine. Place the text inside the rectangle you drew earlier. When you complete the process, your screenshot will be as follows.

Lesson 6: Nested Ring Magnet Design

In this lesson, you will learn to design a magnet with 2 interlocking rings. Tools and techniques to be used in this course are used in many jobs. That's why you should learn these tools well. Let's start the lesson immediately.

First, take the ellipse draw tool in the toolbar on the left and draw a circle while holding down the CTRL-key. Then, while holding the dimensioning corners of the circle you draw and holding the SHIFT key, slide the mouse inwards and create another circle with the left click. If you want, you can draw another circle in the circle you created instead of doing this operation. If you learn the method I told you first, you can do your work faster and properly. Select these two circles and click on the COMBINE tool in the top toolbar. Thus, you will have created a single object. Copy one of this object you created into a blank space. Make the second object you copied slightly smaller than the other. These two objects will be a man and a woman ring. When you complete the process, your screenshot should be as follows.

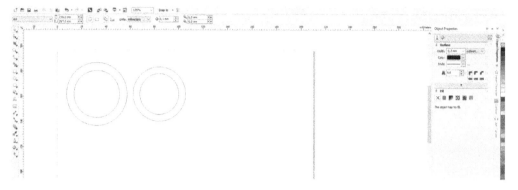

After this step, place the small object on the large object so that some amount comes out. Your screenshot should be as follows.

Then select both objects and click on the WELD tool at the top so that both circles will merge to form a single object. After completing this process, draw a square on a blank area and get the shape tool. We will draw a diamond figure on this square women's ring. After drawing the square, select the square and press CTRL + Q or click Convert To Curves from the ARRANGE menu. And click on the shape tool your screenshot should be as below.

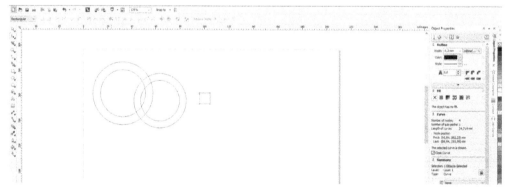

As you can see in the picture, blue dots should appear on all four corners of the square. You can shape the square by holding these points. If you hold down the SHIFT key after holding each point, you can only move it to the right or the top and down. This might work for you. Create a shape using the dots as shown below.

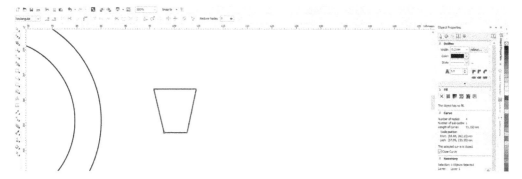

With the Shape tool still selected, double click anywhere on the top line of this shape you created and create another point. Drag this point you created to an area as shown below and use only the mouse to do this drag.

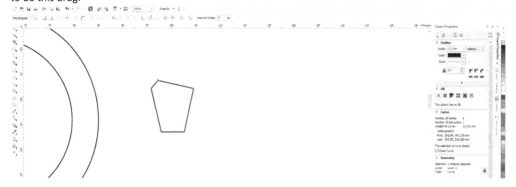

Repeat the process for the line to the right of the point you created and drag the point to a location as you see below.

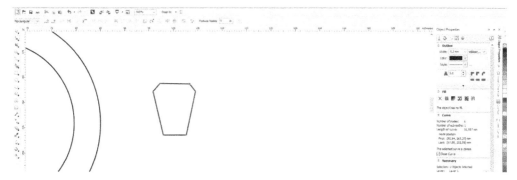

Thus, you will have drawn the exterior of the diamond figure. After this stage, you will need to use a new vehicle. The name of this vehicle is PEN TOOL. As you can see below, you can access this tool by right-clicking or long-clicking the icon on the toolbar on the left. We will continue our process by taking the Pen tool.

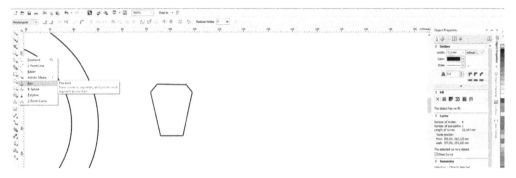

With this tool, we will make a few drawings to make the diamond figure you draw more realistic. Pen tool draws a straight line between both points you click. Draw the shapes you see below into the shape you draw using this tool.

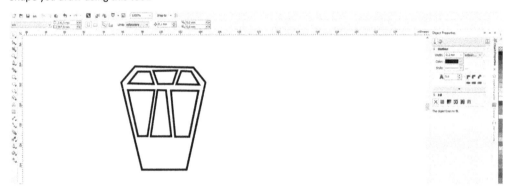

Feel free to draw incorrectly After completing your drawing, click on each object using the shape tool and make any corrections you want from the blue dots in the corners. Make it more symmetrical. As a result, your drawing should look like the following.

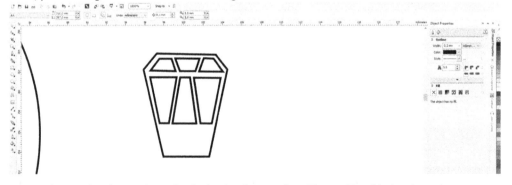

It is enough to have a shape that looks visually smoother. After making this drawing, take your diamond drawing with the drawings in it and place it in a small amount over the small circle. Then rotate the shape according to the position of the ring by clicking on the object once more or by entering a value in the rotation area at the top. When the process ends, your screenshot should be as follows.

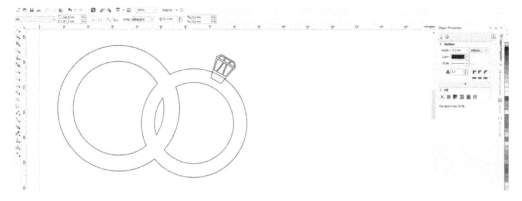

After this stage, just click once on the outline of the diamond figure you drew. Then, while holding down the SHIFT key, click the circle once and click on the WELD tool. This process will combine diamonds and rings. Your screenshot will be as follows.

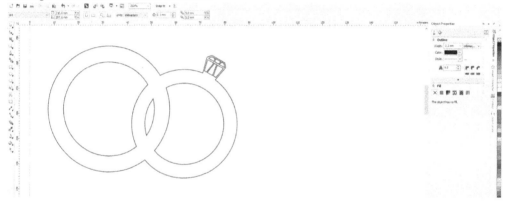

We have completed the ring design, you can now draw a rectangle inside the ring shape or under these objects and write whatever you want in this rectangle. First, let's write on the inside of the ring. First, write the text you want to write using a small font. Then select the text with the Selection tool and choose the Fit Text To Path option from the TEXT menu and place the pointer over the ring, you will get an image as you see below.

You can make placement by clicking the mouse once in a part you deem appropriate. Let's move on to the other option.

In this option, take the rectangle drawing tool from the toolbar on the left and draw a slightly shorter rectangle based on the size of both rings. Then enter a value in the corner rounding section on the toolbar at the top, rounding the corners. Write the article you want to write in a separate section. Place the rectangle just enough to overlap the bottom of the rings. Click once on the ring shape. Press and hold the SHIFT key and click once on the newly drawn rectangle shape and click the WELD tool to combine the shapes. Then complete the drawing by placing the text you wrote in the rectangle. When you do these operations, your screenshot will be as follows.

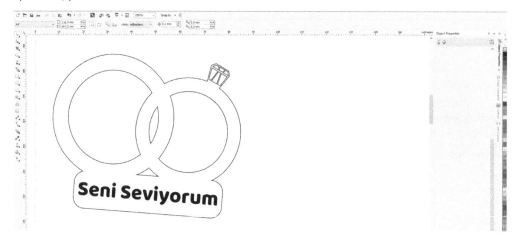

Lesson 7: Making Magnets by Downloading and Editing Stock Vector

In this lesson, we will download a ready-made vector file over the internet and draw a magnet drawing. Thus, you will learn to use the vectors you download from the internet and prepare these vectors for laser cutting. The website we will use is www.freepik.com . First of all, you should find a vector drawing suitable for the magnet you will design. I found a vector for you, you can download it from the link below and download it for free. First, drag and drop the EPS file in the file you downloaded into our program. You will see an image like the one below.

Vector Drawing Link: https://www.freepik.com/free-vector/vintage-design-ornamental-frame-collection_5533897.htm

A menu with the image import options you see. Just apply the settings in the picture you see here. Briefly, these are settings that allow you to import editable and import text as shapes. After making the selections here, press OK. Depending on the size and complexity of the vector drawing, it may take several minutes to arrive on your screen. At this stage, I recommend you not to use the program without drawing. The reason is that at this time, the program may become unresponsive and shut down.

After the vector drawing is reflected on your screen, you should distribute the group of this drawing. This is because there is more than one object in the drawing. To get the only drawing you need, you should use the group dispatch tool in the top toolbar. First, select the drawing and click on UNGROUP ALL ( ) in the top toolbar. If you select the sample stock vector that I provided after these operations, the screenshot will be as below.

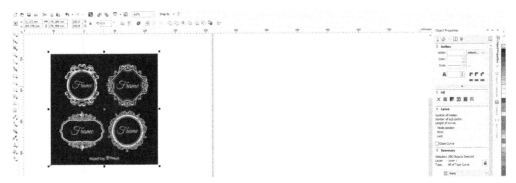

We will use the drawing in the upper left corner. To do this, select the vector drawing you will use starting from a blank area and move it to another area. You can delete other vectors. We need to make changes to this vector you bought. First, you should make the outline of the vector hairline and fill no fill, then the screenshot should be as below.

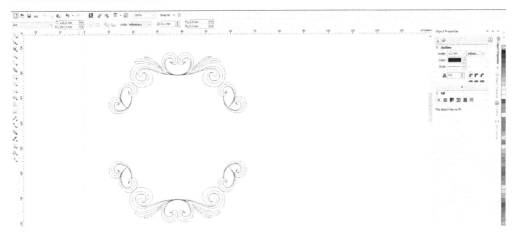

In this drawing, the part that will be needed for us is the decorative part, which is drawn in black on the upper side, and the rest of it is selected one by one. The screenshot will be as follows.

As you can see, there are smaller objects inside this object and each object is independent. Erase what is inside from these objects and place them on top of each other so that they can be a single object. You can see the small objects first after they are deleted and the objects placed on top of each other below.

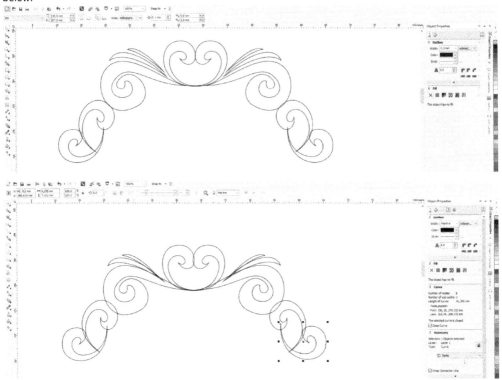

After completing these operations, use the WELD tool by selecting all the objects and your screenshot should be as follows.

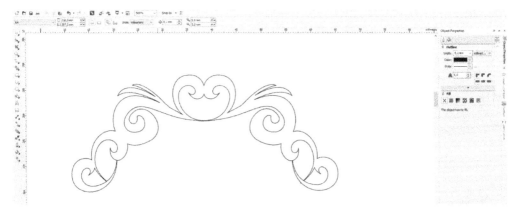

Now draw a circle so that it can overlap the lower parts of this object and copy one from this object to the bottom of the circle. After you move the object, you can copy with the right click without releasing the mouse. I share the screenshot below.

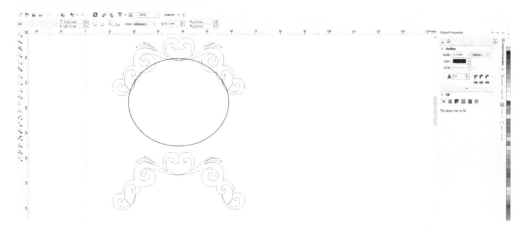

Reverse the other object you copied below vertically with the Mirror Vertically ( ) tool in the top toolbar. Move this drawing to the top of the circle, just like the drawing at the top. Draw a smaller circle inside the circle you draw and write the text you want. Select the objects in the big circle, upper and lower parts one by one by pressing the SHIFT key and use the WELD tool. After the operations, your screenshot will be as follows and your magnet design will be ready.

Lesson 8: Simple Wall Clock Design

In this section, we will design a simple wall clock. First, draw a rectangle on a blank document and draw a square of 300 millimeters by 300 millimeters. Then roll the corners with the tool at the top that we showed in the previous sections. Then your screenshot should be as below.

Then you should prepare a guide to place the numbers, one of the most important parts of the watch design. To do this, first select the straight line tool.

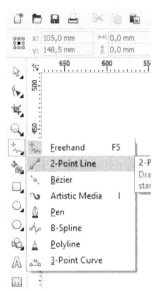

After selecting the tool you see on the left, click on an empty part and hold down the SHIFT key while pulling. Create a long straight line. Once you have selected this line, click on it once and hold it with a mouse from any of the flip icons around it. Start turning by holding down the CTRL-key. After 2 steps turn, copy 1 with the right mouse button. Then select the line you copied and copy the process until you complete the circle with the CTRL + R key on the keyboard. Each line in this process will be the measurements of the numbers of the clock. The final version of your drawing should look like the image below.

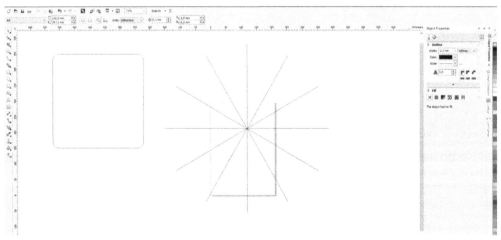

Once you have reached this stage, select all the lines and group them with the toolbar at the top or CTRL + G keys. Select the group that you previously drawn with the grouped lines and press C and E respectively. This will align the centers of both objects. After this alignment, the places where you will place the numbers will be exactly specified. In each empty space, write each digit of the watch separately. You can set the font and size you want. Make sure that each number is written separately.

Then, holding these posts by their center points, align them with the line above each where they should be. While doing this process, it will be sufficient to adjust the distance of the numbers out of the square to make an eye decision. After aligning all the numbers, your screenshot should be as follows.

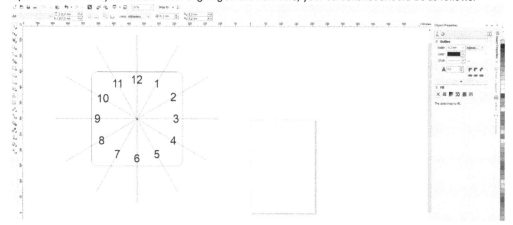

A tip that will make your job easier: when aligning the numbers, make sure that one and five and two and four are aligned, and five and seven and four and eight are aligned. The same alignment process will be the same for the number directly opposite or next to the other numbers, making the watch look more beautiful. You can do this by moving the numbers with the SHIFT key and then changing the number. After these operations, all you have to do is open the hole where you will place the clock mechanism and this hole size may change. However, the most used size is 9mm in diameter. Take the Ellipse tool and press the CRTL key to draw a circle, and then adjust its dimensions to be 9 mm. Select the circle you draw and the base of the clock and press C and E respectively. Then delete the alignment lines. Thus, you will have made the first watch design. Your screenshot should be as follows.

Lesson 9: Butterfly Cut Wall Clock Design

In this section, you will learn a more beautiful looking wall clock design. First, the base of this wall clock will be a circle. Open a blank worksheet and, after taking the ellipse tool, hold down the CTRL key and draw a 300-millimeter circle. After drawing this circle, prepare a dimension line as described in the previous section. If you don't want to prepare this dimension line every time, just draw and save the dimension line in an empty file. You can import and use it when you are drawing a clock. After performing the operations I mentioned, your screenshot should be as follows.

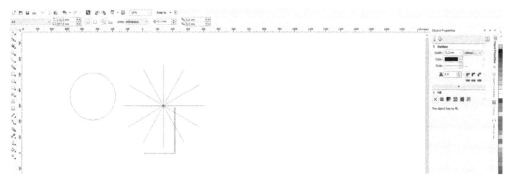

After this stage, group the lines as described in the previous section. Select both objects and press C and E respectively. After aligning the objects, write the desired font and numbers and align them on the lines. Then draw the clock mechanism hole with a diameter of 9 millimeters. Select the base of the watch and the hole you drew and align with the C and E keys respectively. Delete your dimension lines. I explained it quickly because the transactions up to this point are the same as the previous section. When all these operations are done, your screenshot will be as follows.

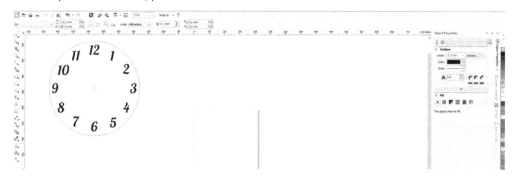

Next is to decorate the clock design with butterflies. Download a butterfly vector online. You can use the www.flaticon.com site for this process. I will share the link of the vector drawing that I will use in this section.

Link: https://www.flaticon.com/free-icon/butterfly-shape-top-view_42499?term=butterfly%20silhouette&page=1&position=3

Download the vector drawing on the link as an SVG file and drag it into the program. The drawing you downloaded should look like the following.

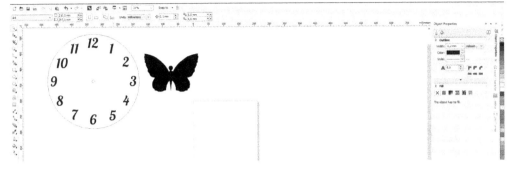

Select the butterfly drawing you downloaded and select its outline as a hairline on the right. In the filling section, select the no fill option. Then delete the number 1 on the clock and copy and place the butterfly by adjusting the size and turning it a little. Then your screenshot should be as below.

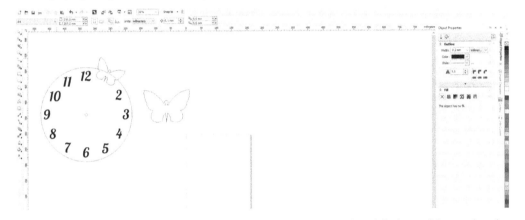

After doing this operation, select the butterfly placed on the watch and the base of the watch and click on the Back Minus Front ( ) tool. Then the clock base will be cut according to the shape of the butterfly and your peer image will be as follows.

The rest of the procedures are quite easy. Copy the butterfly shape in different sizes and angles from the blank area. If you wish, you can place it inside and outside the watch. The final drawing of your watch should be as follows.

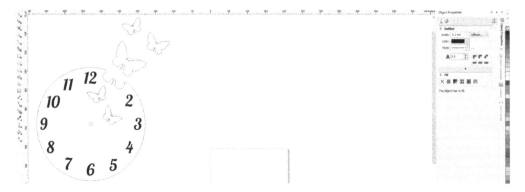

Lesson 10: Wall Clock Design with Roman Numerals

In this section, we will design a watch with roman numerals that have a more authentic look. First, open a blank worksheet and this time draw a 200-millimeter circle with the ellipse draw tool. Then create your dimension lines described in the previous sections and place them in the circle with the C and E keys. Write the Roman numerals separately in another blank space using the letters "I" "X" "V". Then your screenshot should be as below.

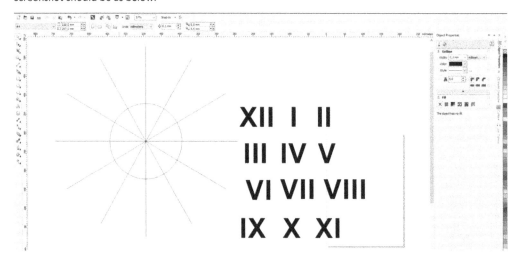

After typing the numbers, you can take the shape tool and adjust the spaces between them. You can also reduce the font sizes to fit around the circle. Place the numbers around the circle to match the shape. When placing, make sure that the numbers are straight and legible. The numbers should be placed over the circle you draw. When the process is completed, the screenshot will be as follows.

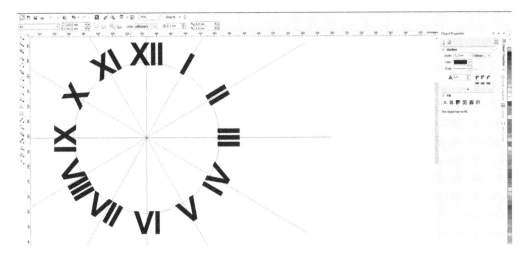

After this step, delete the guidelines. Draw a slightly smaller circle inside the circle you draw. Draw a large circle with the outer parts of the numbers and draw a larger circle from that circle. After drawing these circles, your screenshot should be as follows.

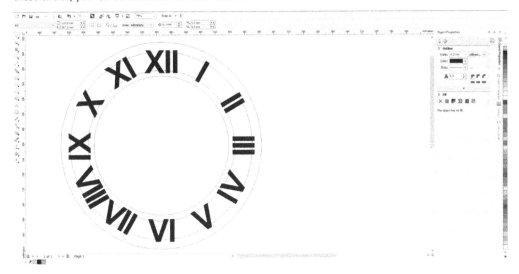

Very little action left. Select the two small circles you draw inside and click on the combine ( ) tool. Then select the two large circles you draw on the outside and click on the combine tool again. After all these operations, select all objects and click on the weld ( ) tool. Thus, your clock drawing will be completed. To place the mechanism of your watch, you can copy 1 more from the outermost large circle and use it as a base. If you wish, you can place the mechanism separately on the wall. Your screenshot should be as follows.

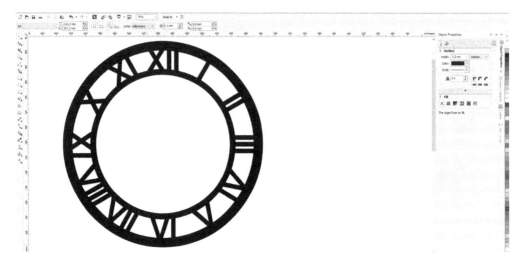

Lesson 11: Mixed Shape Wall Clock Design

In this section, you will learn to design a wall clock with a mixed shape. As usual, open a blank worksheet first. Draw a full 150-millimeter circle with the Ellipse tool. It is important that the circle is small so that the clock looks beautiful. In another blank part, create clock guides and the bore of the mechanism. Write only the numbers "12", "3", "6" and "9" with the fonts you want and place them on the outside of the circle. The numbers must be large in size. Your screenshot should be as follows.

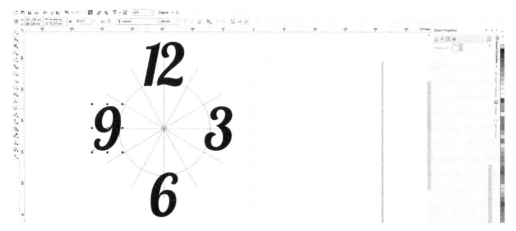

Make sure that each number is placed slightly over the circle. You can now write other numbers. Write the other numbers in a blank space and start placing them in order. You can change the size and direction of the numbers as you like during the placement. This will make your watch look more unusual. The image below shows the placement of the number "1".

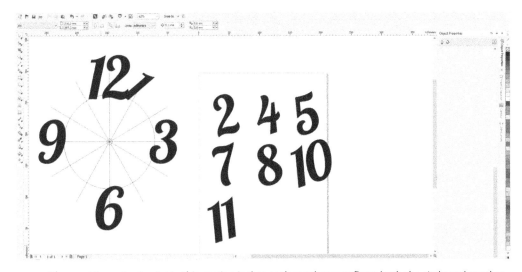

The most important point in this section is that each number overflows both the circle and another number. In this way, the watch will be both solid and beautiful. Place other digits as you wish, respectively. Below you will see all the numbers placed.

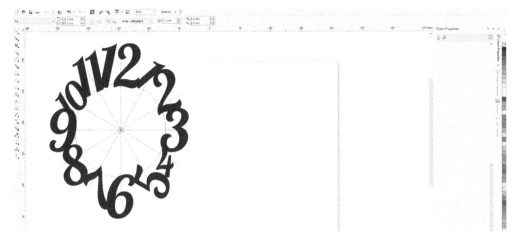

Delete the grid lines. Select all objects except the hole you drew for the mechanism and combine all objects with the weld ( ) tool. The final version of your drawing will be as follows.

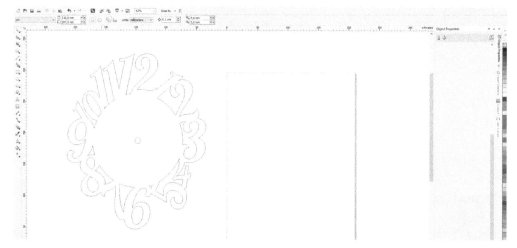

All that remains is to create a nail hole to hang your watch on the wall. The reason for creating a hanging hole on this watch is not to encounter balance problems caused by the shape of the watch. Draw a circle with a diameter of 5 millimeters. Draw a 10-millimeter circle outside of this circle and combine these two circles using the combine tool. Then place this object on a place that coincides with the time you drew. Select the object and the outline of your watch and press the C key. This will align your watch and the nail hole you draw vertically. Then hold the nail hole and press the SHIFT key and slide it over the clock. Drag enough over the outside of the watch's outline. Then select the outer line and nail hole of your watch and click on the weld tool. Thus, the drawing of your watch will be completed. The screenshot should be as follows.

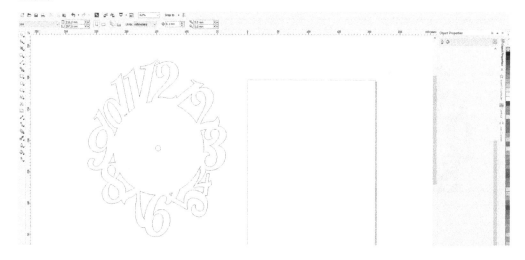

Result

Our lessons in this book ends here. Of course, this is not the first and last book, and my new books with many different laser cutting applications are on the way. I have already started to write my book, where you can find drawings of different products. All of them will have designs that will work for you and you will use a lot. If you have any drawing samples you would like to see in my books, I would like you to send them to me at mrgraphizm@gmail.com. Also, don't forget to rate my book on Amazon. Your comments and suggestions are very important to me.

In my other books, there will be many examples such as bookmarks, objects you can use on special occasions, invitations you can make with laser cutting, kitchen ornaments, cake ornaments. Thank you very much for your interest in the pre-order of my book. Hope to see you in my next book. Take care, my friends.

Abdulkadir Kaşoğlu.

www.ingramcontent.com/pod-product-compliance
Lightning Source LLC
LaVergne TN
LVHW041207050326
832903LV00020B/515